Coming Home

By Adina Brown

Library For All Ltd.

LIBRARY FOR ALL

DIGITAL EDUCATION · FOR THE WORLD

Library For All is an Australian not for profit organisation with a mission to make knowledge accessible to all via an innovative digital library solution. Visit us at libraryforall.org

Coming Home

First published 2023

Published by Library For All Ltd
Email: info@libraryforall.org
URL: libraryforall.org

Our Yarning logo design by Jason Lee, Bidjipidji Art

Original illustrations by Fariza Dzatalin Nurtsani

Coming Home
Brown, Adina
ISBN: 978-1-922991-04-1
SKU03438

Coming Home

We respect and honour Aboriginal and Torres Strait Islander Elders past, present and future. We acknowledge the stories, traditions and living cultures of Aboriginal and Torres Strait Islander peoples on this land and commit to building a brighter future together.

One day Adina came home from school upset.

She told her mum she felt like something was missing inside her.

Mum said, "I know exactly how to fix that."

"Come on bub, jump in the car. I know what will help."

Boom, boom! They got in the car and drove for a long, long time.

Suddenly, Andina knew where they were going.

To the beach, but not just any beach — Forster Beach.

Forster Beach: her mum's Country.

Forster Beach is where her mum, grandma and great gran all go to connect to Country and feel alive.

"Ahh, Biripi Country," Mum sighs, and smiles as Adina breathes the sea air in and out, laughing happily.

Adina wiggled her toes in the sand. A whirl of wind blowing in her hair, she began to feel good.

Adina smiled at her mum.

Later that night, on the beach sitting around the campfire with her mob, she knew her mum was right.

Coming home onto Country made her feel warm and happy.

You can use these questions to talk about this book with your family, friends and teachers.

What did you learn from this book?

Describe this book in one word. Funny? Scary? Colourful? Interesting?

How did this book make you feel when you finished reading it?

What was your favourite part of this book?

download our reader app
getlibraryforall.org

About the author

Adina is from the Gumbaynggirr/Biripi and Yuin Nations and lives in Canberra. She loves campfires and painting with her dad. Her favourite story when she was little was *How the Birds Got Their Colours*.

Our Yarning

Want to discover more books from this collection? Our Yarning is a collection of books written by Aboriginal and Torres Strait Islander peoples across Australia.

We know that children learn better, and enjoy reading more, when they see themselves in the stories, characters and illustrations of the books they read.

To download the app, visit the Google Play Store on any Android device and search 'Our Yarning'.